VIA Folios 141

Journeys on the Wheel

Journeys on the Wheel

B. Amore

BORDIGHERA PRESS

© 2020 by B. Amore

Library of Congress Control Number: 2019943039

Cover design by Winslow Colwell/Wren Song Design

Artwork by Zannah Noe, *Cloud Painting with Laser etched Ferris Wheel*
zannahnoe.com

All rights reserved. Parts of this book may be reprinted only by written permission from the author, and may not be reproduced for publication in book, magazine, or electronic media of any kind, except for purposes of literary review by critics.

Printed in the United States.

Published by
BORDIGHERA PRESS
John D. Calandra Italian American Institute
25 West 43rd Street, 17th Floor
New York, NY 10036

VIA Folios 141
ISBN 978-1-59954-146-4

CONTENTS

I: *Queries*
15 What's the Hurry?
17 Surrender
18 Due Stelle
21 99 Cent Dreams
23 Catching Up
25 Dear Diary
27 Swallow, Suck, Breathe
29 St. Mary's Church
31 Papa Nonno
33 Mother Ache
34 The Women Remember

II: *Ruminations*
37 Night of First Snow
38 An Act of Faith
39 On Hatred
40 Great Blue Heron
41 Loathe to Leave
42 Ballad of the Pans
45 *Il Giardino*
47 November 6
49 Mother
50 The Trailer
52 Too American
54 Dropped Stitch
56 Apparition
58 Condor to Border

III: *Memories*
63 What Do I See?
65 Longing
66 "A Memory, a Monologue, a Rant, and a Prayer"
68 Family Kitchen
70 Feeding the Birds
72 Heading for the Butter and the Royal Lunch
74 In Those Days, We Were Naked, Clothed

78 Sphere of Bone
79 Portrait: Annie, in America
80 Lament
82 God Given Talent

IV: *Insights*

87 Tangerine Memories
89 Sundays
90 Healing
92 The Lake in Winter
93 Requiem for Tsunami Dead
94 All Hallow's Eve Reverie
95 The Village Woman
96 Circle of Bodies
98 The Earth
99 Baby Bird
102 *Gemelle*
104 On Seeing My Mother's Dresser at Easter
106 Time of the Turtles

V: *Reflections*

109 High Desert
110 Keeping Company
112 Voice
113 Living the Question
114 The Everpresent Eye of God
115 A Kiss on the Lips
118 "Where's Annie?"
120 Anointed
122 The Days Are Lost, Counting
123 Night Kitten
124 Interlude
125 Wheel

ACKNOWLEDGMENTS
ABOUT THE AUTHOR

*In gratitude for the creative spirit
which inspires each day
with the breath of life*

Be patient toward all that is unsolved in your heart
And try to love the questions themselves
Do not seek the answers that cannot be given to you
Because you would not be able to live them
And the point is to live everything
Live the questions now
Perhaps you will without noticing it
Live along some distant day into the answers

RAINER MARIA RILKE

I: *Queries*

WHAT'S THE HURRY?

Turtle-like the officer blinks his eyes,
head large through my open window,
"License and registration, ma'am."

Already prepared they fit into his square hand.
He ambles slowly back to his black shell
blue light flashing its warning to others,
semi-numbed by the road,
still easing their way down the mountain.

I, abruptly halted in mid-rise,
between two peaks,
wait and wait and wait.

Slowly he lumbers back.
"Got to ask you a question, might seem odd—
Are you in the military?"
Then, with surprise, "You have a perfect record."
"Yes, I'm careful."

Care full
Full of cares
Too many jostling for consideration

II

Drive time, dream time,
settling in for the long haul.
Time stands still.
One lane only, no choice but to follow.

Rain, sleet, roadwork, trucks.
I ruminate—one hundred seventy eight dollars,
remembering his dark hooded turtle eyes,
slow speech, "Ma'am, what's the hurry?"

An old Italian proverb comes to mind,
"He who rushes meets death more quickly"

III

Rain slants, heavy on the glass.
I stare through slits as if the light of sight
could penetrate more deeply
into the question of this night.

Turtle floats, dives, disappears
Ripples skim silvered surface
Light holds the center
Eyes rise—slowly blink
"What's the hurry?"

SURRENDER

There's nothing
like being sick,

the inner dialogue
to do or not to do
suddenly reduced.

Even regret retreats.

Patience and plenitude
fill my burning body
in the morning hours
of a sleepless night.

Scenes from this lifetime
pass like lantern slides
viewed at a distance,

the fever
burning them all to ash
as I relearn the meaning
of surrender.

DUE STELLE

Due stelle son' cadute mezzo o' mare
Due stelle 'nnamorate e 'sto paese
A do' si ride e chiagne tutt a' vita
A do' l'ammore fa mori' o' campà

Two stars have fallen into the sea
Two stars in love with this place
where you laugh and cry all your life
where love makes you live or die.

I

Were they twin souls as the song says?
Is that why she loved the words so,
as she played the recording over and over,
a woman of thirty-nine with
four children and devoted husband.

I'm thirteen. My mother is finally
back from Italy, her first trip
since she left as a child,
thirty two years before.

Every day, letters begin to arrive,
soft blue paper, flowing writing.

Replies, penned in my mother's
inimitable script, also blue ink on blue paper.

Those letters haunted the days.
Soulful Neapolitan ballads filled the
heavy night air in my father's absence,
as he dutifully worked two jobs with
the family safely tucked into beds.

II

She, the romantic dreamer,
re-enamoured of the Italy
she had lost as a child.
Did she love the Italian man,
or Italy through him?

He showed her Naples,
sipping octopus soup at
midnight in the fish market
of Porta Capuana,
the Vomero under starlight,
lovers at Parco della Rimembranza in
cars with newspaper-curtained windows.

He, a poet of Naples, wrote love songs for a city,
city becoming lover, lover becoming Italy.
Where were the lines of boundary?
Four children between the lines.

She said that is why she didn't stay,
that is why she didn't leave,
not because of the two-job,
faithful, philosopher-husband.

III

Subsequent trips, alone,
for relief of her "nerves."
Long absences from lonely children.

In photos, the round stone Trulli of
Alberobello shine, whitewashed, magical,
with their domed slate roofs.

She is tanned, smiling, with him beside her,
also smiling.

Was it love? Love for him that drew her?
Love for the little ones that brought her home?
And love for patient husband?

She, always the idol,
revered like the Virgin Mary,
never pretended to be a saint,
kept her silence,
clues read into the empty spaces
between the lines.

IV

Later—witnessing a first meeting
of him and my father, I was surprised
at how alike they were.

Playing chess at the kitchen table
discussing philosophy, drinking wine
laughing together.

Born on opposite sides
of a broad ocean,
brought together by
love of the same
woman.

99 CENT DREAMS

"The only thing she's good for
is to have a good time,"
he mutters as we pass a
young woman wearing the
shortest short shorts
I have ever seen.

My taxi driver is handsome,
majoring in finance and
economics, saving all
his textbooks, he tells me
in perfect English—then
continues whispering
another language
into his hanging phone mike
as we thread through
dense New York streets.

Under a Lexan case
hung on a brick building,
Jesus, in red robes,
with outstretched
arms, is embracing
the whole scene—

A homeless woman
screams "Freddie"
    into the air,

Art students carrying
stretched canvasses,
move en masse
across 23rd Street,
oblivious to the stream of
rush hour traffic,

The man with a crushed
Anthony Quinn face and
five foot body, is lost in his
own ruminations.

Faces, faces, faces—
every variation of
success and failure;
the American experiment
parading before the eye.

Every person moving,
step by step,
along the journey of
their lives past a
store called
99 Cent dreams.

CATCHING UP

The red-haired mailman Ed
stops to chat.
We catch up on the news,
two close family members with cancer,
brother in law with a stroke,
my husband's surgery.

But what brings me to tears as
we stand in the grey gravel drive,
is the news of his brother's son,
only twenty years old,
who fell off a building during
spring break in Fort Lauderdale.

Probably drinking.
Maybe even something more.
We both nod sympathetically,
our eyes meeting as
we acknowledge the painful
truths of youth.

Weeks later as I'm driving at dusk,
a deer runs out of the woods to my right.
Again, in an instant impossible to foresee,
life turns to death.

The constable who comes is matter of fact
as he drags the carcass to the side of the road.
I'm still in shock wondering
why there's no warning sign.

The next day I remember Ed's grey blue eyes
looking into mine on that quiet morning
in late summer when we shared

our deepest griefs of the past year.
His still present sadness
thickening his generally cheery voice,
my quick tears for a boy I never met,
for my daughter, brother, husband,
welling up unforeseen
with the morning mail.

DEAR DIARY

You've grown up, changed form
no longer bound in gold-embossed blue leather
and fitted with a diminutive lock and key.

The days are long gone when your
cream-colored pages with thin pale lines
neatly contained days and weeks
filled with unruly meanderings of
teenage dreams.

Today you've changed your name
just as I did at fifty,
when deciding to let go of ten letters.
It was a great relief,
when seeing the shorter version,
not to be reminded of so much
that I could never write
in your tiny cramped pages,
so much that I truly never wanted
anyone else to know,
so much that I didn't know myself
for too many years.

Today I call you journal.
Sturdy, with your strong spiral spine,
you are my most trusted friend.
I love the whiteness of your blank pages,
spread so evenly beneath my yellow
number 2 Pentel mechanical pencil,
tracing words that slip with ease
between my morning mind and
your pages waiting to be filled.

Do you like it when I feed you words and thoughts?
You're pretty passive until I've written
what I can barely say aloud.
You often help me think things through,
work out my most conflicted feelings.

Then your pages are electric with the crackle
of contrary thoughts seeking modest resolution,
or my sense of hopelessness that I will ever find one,
or my fantasies of alternate improbabilities that somehow
assuage the inner anguish of questions still alive,
like how I could again have chosen a partner
so like my father in all the most important ways,
constant and distant in the same moment.

You've become the unedited book of my life,
collecting the dawn jottings of poems,
the stories that have their beginnings in your pages,
the laundry lists of to do's that keep my personal,
professional, and household days in order.

It's been over thirty years
and I'm becoming ever more attached to you.
If all your pages were collected you'd fill a large wall.
Sometimes I wonder if when I'm older,
I'd be curious enough to read a bit of you each day
like the Russian novels that fill my winter months.

You would go on and on and I wonder if I would
see any changes in the questions or characters or
would the stories repeat themselves.

Well, hopefully there are more years
of pages to fill on other sleepless nights.
I don't yet know how the story turns out.
Do you?

SWALLOW, SUCK, BREATHE

Still tiny,
yet determined,
you insist on your
own rhythm.

Sucking so strongly
until satiated
that I stare in
wonder,

marveling at the life force,
fiercely persistent,
that has brought you
here.

How hard we had to try
to learn the patience
to allow you
to find your own pace.

You root and fret still,
as if in fear that
sustenance will not
come.

When I see your sliver
of a smile at feeding's end,
I sense a growing trust
that there will be enough.

My lips touch
the soft top of your
head as I hold you
upright.

You stir before
settling in
to sleep,

that slight tremor
of a smile
carrying you
into dreams.

ST. MARY'S CHURCH

My father had been an altar boy
at St. Mary's Church
in Boston's North End.

When the church was torn down,
I saved a piece, brown limestone,
rough, rectangular, grainy.

I always wanted to carve
a St. Thomas for him—started
with a feeling but no clear vision,

put the praying gesture of supplication
into the form, smoothed the head
and praying hands but got
no further.

It sits in my studio, nearly thirty years
after the fact, and I still wonder
that I never gave it to him.

Even unfinished,
he'd probably
have loved it.

It could have lived happily in his
garden amidst my mother's roses
and his basil plants,

an indeterminate touchstone, just
mysterious enough to have fit
into his contemplative life.

Now he is gone. St. Thomas remains.
I wonder why I never told my father
of my desire to please him,
and of my failed attempt.

PAPA NONNO

I lie here in Vermont dreaming of you
your stout strong frame
muscular even in old age
the wrinkles of your face
set like the lines of a map

Your progeny now criss-cross the globe
What would you think of the
multitude of grandchildren,
and great, great grandchildren
two in far away Singapore,
and others in the Italy you left
more than a hundred years ago,
children of the children of a
daughter who returned

Would you feel your dreams fulfilled
after a lifetime of digging tunnels,
building granite walls

Would you feel that we have
honored your life's work

Would we make you proud
some of us with university degrees,
some of us studying still

You who never returned to
the village of your birth

You the man who signed a humble X
on your request to remain in your
chosen country

You who filled a pained tooth
with cement from your job

You who snarled at any provocation and
prodded us as children with your cane
when we passed by your chair

You, stout strong tough old grandfather
stubborn as you had to be to survive
as hardworking as you had to be
to feed your many children
as tied to tradition as you chose to be
continuing to make wine every autumn
despite your new country's laws

You who nurtured your tomato plants
on your belly, pulling yourself along
with those strong pick and shovel arms
when your knees had finally said
enough

You, grandfather, who gave us life
thank you, and in your own tongue
grazie, little man
from the south of Italy
still sending up shoots

MOTHER-ACHE

it's 3AM, winter snow has turned to
spring rain despite it's being January still
you are the first thought that comes
in this dark morning-night

the child you were
hunches over in the small crib
the young mother I was,
traces circles, palm flat and soft,
on your little back

now a mother yourself, you lie abed
in a city distant from this country place,
with a body cut and stitched,
the wayward cells
hopefully held at bay

my hand yearns to stretch out, to
offer comfort in the bed where you
sleep with the father of your children

my heart, my feeling heart, aches with
love and longing; the mother urge
so primal—I hold my peace,
you are your own, have always been

I sometimes call; you sometimes share
our caring understood between the lines
of polite question and terse response

I breathe my love into the rain-filled night
praying for your healing and deep rest
suffering with the wish to make it right
knowing you need free space
to find your way to renewed life

THE WOMEN REMEMBER

Graying hair,
generous bodies,
and still we form a ring

Center dance floor
jiggling, laughing
hip swinging, toe strutting
breasts bobbing,
flowing into that rhythm
pumped by the drums

The needle of time swings backwards,
women of another generation,
fuller bodied in longer dresses,
flowered and flowing,
glide more sedately in couples,
twirl magically on the gilded floor,
reveling in the transformation
from kitchen to celebration

Now I've become one of the elders
wearing bright red shoes,
laughing and taking center stage,
with my sister and Regina and Debbie

The men drink and watch
as our bodies slip into
the memory of girlhood and
our mothers, and our grandmothers

The circle widening
and tightening with
every drum beat
of the heart.

II: *Ruminations*

NIGHT OF FIRST SNOW

you came
with a bottle of
deep red wine
in hand

to celebrate
the night of
first snow

falling softly
the flakes blanketed
the browning autumn
earth

for a brief moment
our eyes touched
we smiled

and then slipped
into the familiar
rhythm of
our evenings

forgetting too quickly
the white magic
on the other side
of dark glass

AN ACT OF FAITH

this daily push to the frigid studio
turning on the heat, starting a fire in
the old square-boxed iron stove
veteran of uncounted winters
slow warming of the flesh and psyche
as waves of heat permeate to bone

by the time the largest logs have caught
I am almost ready to begin again
the hopeful exercise of the day
what some call child's play,
creation, or daily art practice

like a Rumi poem, the work spreads
before me and I take it up in the
spirit of the poet meeting his lover

a patient search for just the right touch
that will animate the common elements
of objects, paint and paper
searching, reaching, entering the deep
spirit of effort to transmute the dross
of everyday into what a friend called
art with a capital "A"

by dark, the fire has lost its spark
and I move to bank the coals
storing up some heat for the night ahead
both filled and emptied by hours of work
the spirit stretched and flexed
in unexpected ways

ON HATRED

A familiar face
looks at me as if I don't exist

Where did she learn such lessons?
How is it that the heart
pumping life throughout the body
can turn so against life?

Palestinians immolate themselves to kill Jews
Serbs rape Muslim women
Hutu murder Tutsi and vice versa

Truth and Reconciliation seeks to suture
the wounds of a Nation's war against itself
The Dalai Lama moved Tibet's heart
to Dharamasala

What about the human heart
pumping life
pumping love
pumping hate?

How do we find the center place
where wrongs and wounds are laid to rest
where the breath of every day
subsumes the hurt
and Life again
is pumped
into Life?

GREAT BLUE HERON

I wake—heavy—every morning
The weight of the towers
crashing layer upon layer
collapsing

Yesterday in Benson
A great blue heron
standing still and stately
at the edge of sunken pond

For many minutes—a statue
almost a shadow
mostly seen by his reflection
in the mirror of evening

A sound—and his head and long beak
would slowly rise, listen—
return to watching

I saw this three times
from the bathroom window

I'd started to close down the house
but stopped, fixated on this perfect
miracle of nature
making a visitation

Not daring to move
I watched the glow of setting sun
turn his form to warm copper
tinted blue

Tall heron
Tall towers—catching light
turning color with
tones of sky

LOATHE TO LEAVE

hermit winter holds me hostage
drifted snow muffles the scrape of plough
solitary, the regal red cardinal visits
the weeping cherry every frosty morning
fluttering against the long length of glass
before settling on his curved perch
to take a long look at the wooded house
where humans dwell in warmth

sometimes I stand in the doorway
attempting to return his call
he sits motionless, staring at me,
eye to eye, not moving
I wonder where he spends the rest of the day
while we go about our own necessary tasks
burrowing deep into our winter lives
like silent monks drawn to the white stillness
surrounding the stacked rooms of the quiet house

as I look into the eye of an impending journey
I'm loathe to leave the familiar path
this home warren, seductive in its warmth,
safe in its expected rhythms,
a monastery where the mind
can open, in moments, into its own
expansive universe within the walls
of silence

BALLAD OF THE PANS

Who was she, this woman who
banged on pans outside the window
at the stroke of midnight
on New Year's Eve?

The night was dark, silent.
Streetlights created
soft cones of glow.
Sharp, cold air stung my face.
The thrill of the unexpected
enticed me.

Into the void of black night,
my grandmother sang out
her cacophonous celebration
of the New Year's birth.

She banged the cover
against the pan,
beat it like a drum,
rolled the spoon around inside.

I watched in exalted awe,
wondering what had come into
this generally staid woman.

Given my own small pan and cover,
I joined in the concert,
watching the windows for curious eyes,
but—nothing.
Only our blatant joy
filled the night.

Nonna reveled in our solitude,
sharing her glee with me,
reaching through the
square of black cold
into the wider world.

She seemed crazy sometimes
when she flew into one of her rages,
but tonight she was different.

Let loose, her energy was playful,
not angry. It was one of few
such moments
I ever shared with her.

There was another,
when she waded into the sea,
her dress and apron raised,
silver fish swimming around
her slender white legs,

an unrestrained flash of light,
when the world's eye opened
to new possibility.

I, the first girl-grand-child,
became the repository
of her histories,
her woes,
her joys.

Like the clatter of
New Year's pots,
those deposits have rattled
in my head
for this lifetime.

They can still upset
the balance
of a night's sleep,
causing these words to
spill across the page,

accompanied by her
veined white hands, curly hair,
accented voice, and
beneficent smile.

IL GIARDINO
The Garden *of ancestral land in Lapio, Province of Avellino, Italy*

From the stone house,
the walk down the valley is steep
a cobbled road switches
back and forth

I choose the footpaths
tight to the hillside
between the orchards
and fields

Golden grass beneath
the olives makes a
soft resting place
Ladders, narrow at
the top, lean against
stout trunks

The mother tongue calls
through the valley in the
ancient rhymes and verses
of the ancestors, words
I rarely hear but recognize
instantly

Silvered thin branches
twisted by wind and age
whisper in the language
of my grandmother,
Neapolitan tinged with Spanish,
Greek, and French,
Aggio visto paradiso—
I've seen paradise

In the *Giardino* of our family,
olives roll between my fingers
as between my great grand-father's
as he tested the plumpness
of the yearly harvest

We touch across
a hundred years
His hand and mine
meet on this small plot

Leopardi's *Infinito* echoes
in the silences of the steep valley
il naufragar m'è dolce in questo mare
How sweet to be shipwrecked
in this sea

The view carries the
eye beyond line of sight
into the vastness of a space
denying any notation of time.

This full harvest,
abundant in its fruits,
slakes our thirst
for ancestral earth

Sated, we lie at rest,
merging with the
vines and roots
of olives.

NOVEMBER 6

it's almost over
the 24 hours that
mark your birthday

and still I wish
I could wish you
happy birthday

but you asked
to be allowed to
tiptoe out of my life

and how could I refuse
you whose birthday I
always remember

you whom I married
in our own private ceremony
those decades ago

exchanging amethyst rings
at midnight in the old
18th century Cambridge house

you with whom I
dreamed and traveled

you of the red curls and
gentle laugh

you who brought music
and a soft touch to our lives

you, my soul friend
etched forever in this
lifetime's mirror

you whose birthday
I still remember

MOTHER

I haven't seen my mother
for a long time.

Sometimes she comes in dreams,
her skin soft, white, plump
with its fine, fine wrinkles.

I wake this morning with a longing,
a wish that I could just visit her,
drink a familiar cup of tea
at the kitchen table,
chat about seeming irrelevancies

while all the while taking in her
generous presence, as I watch her
stitch a grandchild's torn shirt,
peering through the
small glasses she used for
detail work.

Sitting across from her,
watching light surround her form,
I begin to enter a timeless space
which feels as if it will go on
forever

my aging and
her absence
disappear in the
shimmering golden glow.

THE TRAILER

They would have loved it
Talked about it for years,
a motor home, filled with
everything you'd need
to live for months
on the road

Vistas opening before the
large slanted front windows
She at the wheel
He looking at spaces
barely imagined except
late at night in his office
overlooking the sleeping city

Always on the obverse schedule
working while others slumbered,
his private dreams lived a
life of their own

Dutiful son, dutiful husband, dutiful father
the second generation urban immigrant
philosopher gazed out of tiered glass,
watching lights, spread across
the quiet city, like bounteous
stars over a desert

Dreaming of Alaska and California
as far from the red brick of Boston
as one could go and still
be in America

Roving in imagination
to explore the land in which
he'd lived but never known

Although he died before the dream
was realized, I like to think that,
in those odd, unfettered moments,

my father became his beloved Ulysses
standing before the sail of the world,
staring into the sea of possibility

TOO AMERICAN

The mother, snub nosed,
chin jutting, arms crossed,
jade bracelet circling
each wrist

Fingering with fascination
a tiny good luck charm
carved in exquisite
detail from a piece
of red hanging coral

The daughter—impassive
to the mother's occasional
question in her country
Chinese

Pretending she
does not hear the
tiny woman with the chopped
off straight black hair and
feet which do not touch
the ground

This bus, too public,
too American—too
many strangers noticing
her mother's strangeness

Too American
for her to admit
that she even understands
the old woman's sing song
chatter

The bus lurches to its
last stop—the mother
nimbly rises, daughter
mirroring the graceful
quick motion

They exit—almost as one body
mother following daughter
not touching—not conversing
the signal intuitively understood

Only after reaching
the broad sidewalk
does the daughter hesitate
for a moment—a flicker of
concern,

Glancing back,
checking that the
older woman had
made it safely down
the deep stairs

They move off,
silent,
side by side

DROPPED STITCH

Row after row,
the needles cross each other,
carrying the yarn, interweaving
the strands

Laborious work,
the attempt to make
each motion carry
the same tension
so that the rows
have an even
knit, purl feel

Sometimes, stopping
to check the pattern,
hand running smoothly
over the soft surface

a hole appears
a dropped stitch,
inadvertent, unseen,
necessitating an
undoing of all
that had been
done

No other choice
if the piece is
to be whole

Talking with you yesterday
brought it all back,
but I finally
think you're right

Better to leave the
past where it lives –
let go,
move on

Like the dropped stitch
the hole you left
still shows up
in the weave

I can't follow back
the strands of our
separate truths,

Can only re-knit
my own piece
so that you have
your place and I
have mine

the private pains
and prayers
made whole
by time

APPARITION

A salesman came
to my door today
smiling his ingratiating
smile through crooked
teeth, some missing
towards the back

A slackness of face,
not unpleasing
relaxed in a way,
folksy, talking about
the neighborhood,
getting to know it,
getting to know us,
selling insurance,
a different kind of
insurance, paid cash,
just right for us,
small business folks,
self employed, sole
support, what would
happen if we got
hurt

Politely, I humored him
a bit but firmly said
my husband would be
more rude, a door
shut in his face
instead of my empathy
with his plight,
this "Willie Loman"
of the endless road,
wrinkled shirt on a

humid day, older car,
grey hair, loose body

Clearly he'd been riding
around knocking on doors
at the end of long country
driveways for some
time

Finally he understood,
despite my genuine civility,
that we would not
become his customers

He slowly ambled
back to the grey sedan
and steered down the drive,
grey blue stone crackling
beneath worn tires

CONDOR TO BORDER

Sweat burns my eyes
as I pick through rubble from
the beach on Condor Street
at the harbor's edge

Shards of pale blue-green glass,
one white and red fishing float,
a grey driftwood frame,
a limp plastic placemat with
its faded sea-colored map

Open water laps the thin pages
of past news, the stories
becoming more mysterious
as the layers float back and
forth over each other

I remember beads of perspiration
on my father's brown forearms
in the family shop on Border Street,
a mile downstream from this
rocky urban beach

Fifty-six years between this moment
and that one, like the opening and
closing of an eyelid

Today, I grimace under rivulets of sweat,
determined to harvest the wasted treasure
of Condor Beach—transform it in my studio
into what I call art

In the dry cleaning shop, he pushed the pedals
of the steam machine, sweat flowing like a river

as he took care not to stain the garment,
newly pressed flat

His shapely muscular legs
stand firm on the stone floor
The dark recess of the shop
opens to the light
of asphalt-paved street
across from the water

His brown eyes look out
in tired but alert question

Why is he still here,
locked into this
dullness of days,
despite his many studies,
shelves of books,
foreign travels

Today, the questions
of his life, unanswered
and silent, still
live within me

His veins crisscross
my own brown hands
as I ponder the taut line
of ongoing reflection
connecting Condor
to Border

III: *Memories*

WHAT DO I SEE?

What is this jumble of mind
as if the strands of life's
weave were loosed,
the regular pattern of knit and purl
surreptitiously interrupted
snipped here and there
in most unexpected places

As pulls of day to day
stretch the fabric more taut
spaces open, gaps appear

What do I see in the interstices?
my mother's ample form
squeezes through,
my brother's pains,
daughter's courage,
husband's illness,
my own breathed fears

Night is filled with
visions between the strands
like a movie continuously
playing, visible only in
the open weave

Still, despite the tugs of
worry widening the holes,
the fabric doesn't give way
but keeps expanding to fit
the changing form that
dreams and waking life create

Images move like light on
water, shimmering slivers
of bright and dark
commingling, like a Monet river
finding its way around a
rustic bend

A slight wind unfetters yellow
leaves that flutter softly
like a shower of butterflies
down into the stream
of birth and death

LONGING

Deep and silent
hidden from sight
solitary, aching
the heart
stretched to bursting in
its sightless cave
sending out
an invisible call,
praying to be heard

Longing
for what is gone
or never was
for what was dreamed
or once held
for what is distant
or one hopes will be

a touch that heals
a soft embrace

"A MEMORY, A MONOLOGUE, A RANT AND A PRAYER" V DAY CELEBRATION, 2012, CAMBRIDGE, MA

The woman stands,
graceful in tall heels,
an elegant black dress
flowing over her slender body,
and shapely legs.

Around her neck,
one circle of red thread
with a single silver bead,
punctuates the austere form
of her figure posed
against the crimson backdrop
of the improvised stage.

The gallery is quiet,
all eyes and lights on her
as she begins
to speak the truth
of her monologue's character,
delineating the images
with stark words.

She spits them out –
rage palpable as she limns
the realities of the women
and girls, put down,
forced down,
denied.

She utters the words
intentionally, slowly, rapidly,
begging her listeners
to actually listen,

pay attention,
do something.
Her voice penetrates
through thick layers,
into the soul.

The audience erupts,
their hands like drumbeats.

Her rant, her rave,
become a prayer
for compassion,
for salvation.

Her plea
cannot
be
ignored.

FAMILY KITCHEN
One Act through Seven Doors

Mannaggia la miseria! Figlia di puttana! Son of a bitch!
Damn Poverty! Daughter of a whore!
Vehement emphasis on the first syllable makes
the swears even more potent.
Words forbidden in my mother's house
are flung with rageful pleasure in the
home of my father's family.

The square kitchen, like the village *piazza* is
the place of gathering and dispute with
lines of passage in constant interplay
as the characters enter and exit
the seven doorways.

Dishcloth in hand, plate half dry,
my grandmother stands firm in the pantry doorway.
Daylight illuminates her regal head of braided silver hair.
Lips, curling around heavily accented words,
hurl a challenge into the open quadrangle
of the room.

Auntie Mary of the shapely legs
and lava-like temper enters from the open door
of her bedroom exclaiming, "You betcha!"
as she plunges into the brewing fray.

Men, gathered round the table, hardly deign to notice.
Their poker game spreads over the oilcloth surface
patterned by mounds of pennies and flashing cards.
Only deep voiced Ray flings a seemingly distracted,
yet pointed, offering from the corner where
a door leads to the outside porch.

III: *Memories*

Dolly, stopping in her passage from bath to living room,
condemns the relative in question with such certainty
that unexpected silence vibrates
in the upper reaches of the tall room

—Only for a moment—

Before the infant, wakened by the family fracas,
starts crying in the small side room opposite
the stairwell where the stocky grandfather
emerges from his cellar, giving the final word—
Tutti siam' nati per morire. Ecco il vino!
We're all born to die. Here's the wine!

FEEDING THE BIRDS

Like Francis of Assisi,
she faithfully fed the birds
every morning

Smaller bits, broken from stale bread
were gently flung from the piazza,
down onto the flat gravel and tar roof
of the downstairs apartment

Deep black in the morning sun,
it was a perfect feeding spot
Even I, short as I was, couldn't miss
the broad plane when I stood beside Nonna,
flinging my own small handfuls in
imitation of her broader gestures

How she enjoyed this generous ritual
Did it remind her of her natal village
in the Irpinian foothills of southern Italy
Did she feel closer to her roots
when beckoning the birds from the branches
of the tall sugar pear tree that rose over the piazza

And come they did, small brown round sparrows,
an occasional black starling or grey pigeon
All feeding peacefully and contentedly at the
wealth of crusty bits freely offered
by the dark haired girl child
and the white-haired woman

She was happy then,
in concert with the world,
the chirping of the sparrows became
the leitmotif of the morning

Petty family squabbles were left behind
within the walls of the large house to our right
We were floating on the piazza's raft,
on a river of air and sunlight,
singing the canticle of Saint Francis,
embracing brother bird and sister sky

HEADING FOR THE BUTTER
AND THE ROYAL LUNCH

I find myself yearning for butter,
the smooth, salty taste on
my tongue, wrapping around
the roof of my mouth—
comforting

Especially when spread on a flat
round, nearly tasteless Royal Lunch
cracker, my mother's favorite

This combo, with a cup of tea
was her panacea for all ills—
the way she would deal with
any bad news

"Let's have a cup of tea"—be it
midnight after a distressing date
or when a letter with unforseen
news arrived in the mail

The ritual was always the same,
reach into the cupboard for the crackers,
set the water to boil, fetch the butter
and milk from the fridge

The familiarity of her response was
soothing, her pillowing form across
the table, a steadying force in a world
which seemed to have temporarily
lost its fragile balance

The simple act of spreading butter
on a cracker, like an answer to a
Zen koan, bringing the wandering
mind back home

IN THOSE DAYS, WE WERE NAKED, CLOTHED
Il primo amore non si scorda mai

I

What would it have been like
to have made love to you then
as many times as I wanted

Desire, like a magnet,
drawing our bodies close
so there was no distance between

Who was the magnet for whom
Who the positive,
Who the negative?

Like those two charged forces,
when in each other's presence, the only
natural thing to do was bond

What if, instead of listening to my
mother, I'd let my hands, arms,
legs wrap around you as
strongly as they wished

What if, I'd taken you inside me,
inside my hungry, desirous inner
mouth

What if, instead of respecting
a certain Catholic distance,
you held me, as close as we both desired

What if, we'd said the deepest
"yes" to each other that we could ?

II

You came to me tonight
in this dream
lifeworn, still beautiful,

My heart quickened to be
walking beside you
I could feel it still—that
gravitational pull of your
nearness

In fits and starts, just as then,
we were near and interrupted
by circumstance

You reached out as if I
would just slip into the
space fitting the curve of
your body

Forty six years later, I am
still unsure
My husband is sleeping
beside me

I'm reticent, you make a small,
sardonic remark, your way
of deflecting pain

How clearly I see it now
as I never did then—and
I am touched to tears

I see you soft, desirous
I see us young, so tenderly
young

I want to give myself to you,
finally acknowledge
how deeply and innocently
we loved each other

I suddenly understand how lovers
destroy lives in the wake
of desire so strong it transcends
decades.

And still, I am not free

III

I regret that I could not
meet you fully as we lay near the sea,
in our bed of crushed long grass
hidden, even from the sharp eyes of gulls,
the sense of Europe's earth shared
between us

Even now, I can feel you pressing
against me, gently stroking,
pushing into my soft, closed thighs

Does that summer breeze of youth
waft only once in a life's time?

IV

*I'm returning now to the dream
and I'm going to hold you as
close as bodies get*

*Skin dissolving until our bones meet
and these two old skeletons
become one.*

*il primo amore non si scorda mai—First love is never forgotten

SPHERE OF BONE

"What's that?"—she
innocently asks
pointing to my bony foot
so different than her own,
so smooth and plump.

What does she see?

the protruding sphere
of bone misshaping
the contour from arch
to tip of big toe,

the crooked little toe
dark, almost hidden
next to its longer
sisters.

In an instant, I see
the years between us,
the days I've spent
walking this lifetime,

We go no further.
The signs of life,
lived, and being lived,
are clear.

Her innocent query
has sharpened the
focus enough
for this
day.

PORTRAIT: ANNIE, IN AMERICA

Summer afternoons under the porch overhang
with my tiny Italian aunt,

Eufrasia of the braided gray bun
and the thin black cotton dress,

who became Annie, in America, but still the
young girl who learned embroidery from the nuns

Taken against her will from the stone village
she made her new home the convent,

teaching her eldest niece in bits and pieces
the minute, precise stitches of her own childhood

Satin thread moves across smooth linen,
silver needle pierces taut surface,
a slight snap with each firm pull sets the stitch
in its proper place

Patiently in and out, around and through,
the Sacred Heart of Jesus takes form and
begins to bleed, the drops formed by
thin white bony fingers

This woman, shriveled into herself,
lines, like a net, crisscross her face,
emotion laced tight within
lips form such a straight line that
the two become one

Only in this tracery of red thread on white ground
does passion give way,

fixing forever the legacy of forbidden emotion
into the knotted heart of memory

LAMENT

Where is peace?

I

Black print vibrates
  on a thin page

ten thousand worlds away
  the news echoes
    through space

II

Walking in
  sunshine

wearing dark plaid
  school uniforms

three Christian school girls
  laughing
    chattering

III

In the reeds
  heads—

thrown like large
  unwieldy
    balls

eyes open
  to the sky

IV

Three young girls less

The Body cries for
  wholeness

Where is Peace?

GOD GIVEN TALENT

in plainspeak, with a matter of fact down east accent
Everard Dallas Hall states, "I'm a gravedigger.
I've got a God-given talent"

with his ready shovel, he's dug over 2,500 graves in
50 years, and photographed each one in winter, spring,
summer, fall, rain or shine

proud of every 4 ½ foot deep, by 8 foot long, by 3 foot wide
cavity that he has wrested from the earth, each the
final cradle for a body now taut with death

the sloping sides, clean corners, carefully mounded
dirt, a meditative practice, grave after grave

it's his matter-of-factness that strikes me as I listen to
the newscast—the straightforward simplicity of his
speech—an acceptance of his life's work

looking it straight in the eye, no illusions
"I've buried my mother, my father, my grandfather,
my two aunts, two uncles and a sister
I'll be starting on my own grave next summer,
I already know the spot," he says, his blue eyes
mirroring the clear, cloudless sky

I've heard the same tone before, in Carrara quarrymen,
in the speech of third generation Campania farmworkers,
a connection so deeply rooted in nature that the words
seem to speak a truth impossible to question

I envy his directness, his acceptance of himself
and how he has lived his life,
so different than mine—
still filled with unanswered questions
and dendrites of doubt

IV: *Insights*

TANGERINE MEMORIES

When I was a child
My grandmother would peel
loose skin off a plump soft
tangerine

Deep orange, oily, it would pull away
from the sweet segments curled
around the secret, open core

Filaments of lighter orange clung
to the inside of each irregular section
of the layer that once protected the fruit

I would marvel that the cobweb threads
which held it fast parted so easily
from the surfaces patterned
by their hold

These rounds of skin, oozing pungent oil,
collected in a small mound
beside Nonna's plate

After the table was cleared and the
kitchen put back in order, she would take
them with me to the dark range oil stove
which warmed and fed the kitchen

Carefully, so as not to burn her fingers,
she would place the largest skins in a
pattern on one of the iron lids holding
the curling blue flames captive in the
belly of the stove

We would sit quietly in two chairs,
one beside the other, one taller,

one small in the silent yellow kitchen,
waiting, everyone else gone to rest
after Sunday dinner

The air, somnolent, thick with a silence
unique to the space usually filled
with movement, waiting,
warmth enveloping us both like
a soft gentle blanket

I would rock back and forth
on my little chair, Nonna's body,
like a large stone, next to me,
still and inward, as magical perfume
began to permeate the air around us

Slowly, as if awakened
from a dream by the alchemy
of soft rinds turning into
hard shells on the hot iron,

Nonna would begin to speak a story,
the story of her youth in a tiny village
surrounded by mountains,
I would become her playmate in the
Giardino of figs and olives

Compatriots, she and I,
in the game of life which transcends time,
Wafting breath of tangerine
lulling us both into the
same dream

SUNDAYS

Do you remember
when we first moved in?
How Sunday afternoons meant
making love on the makeshift
mattress in the corner
of the living room

Somehow I was always
taken by surprise
even though it had
almost become a habit—
the timing, never expected
a look a touch, as quickly
as that we were supine

Afterwards lying close, with
the light from the pond
reflecting off the windows,
we'd doze off, silent and satiated,
burrowed into the nest
our bodies had formed,
slipping into the grace
of Sunday's gift

HEALING

On my knuckle,
first finger of right hand,
a blister, large, round, fat,
full of liquid protecting the
tender flesh below,
burned almost
to bone

For two weeks I've watched
as my body healed itself,
slow and sure

At first, the tender center was
accidentally broken open
over and over,
until a thin skin
finally formed,

every day becoming
a bit more resilient
to the inevitable
encounter which
would re-open
the wound

Then, from edge inward,
each thin line of healing
moving in concentric circles
closer to the center

From depth to surface,
layer by layer,
my skin resolving itself
for fourteen days, tender

to every tacit, unanticipated
touch

Two weeks and two days,
and there is still a slightly
gnarly center where flesh
was once so pained

The last of the crusted scab,
broken open so many times,
is shrinking into oblivion,
slowly closing in on itself

New layers, grown back from
within, cover the bone.
The body's slow, steady
pursuit of well-being
nears completion

I touch a tiny dot
in the center of new, pink skin,
the mountain of my knuckle,
now nearly whole

THE LAKE IN WINTER

Flat expanse of frozen lake
stretches beyond the reach of eye

One tiny dark form
like a Giacometti figure

moves slowly, rhythmically
on its own solitary course

disappears beyond the
curve of cove

Like an apparition, dreamed,
in a moment of reverie,

now, part of the picture plane
painted white

REQUIEM FOR TSUNAMI DEAD

the same waves wash
   all shores

we are not so different
   you and i

rows of bodies
   stretched endlessly

along pale sand
   beaches

along broken
   sidewalks

along hospital corridors
   and in courtyards
      of temples

Buddhist, Muslim,
   Christian, Hindu

the soul knows no name
   as it leaves this earth

becoming a point
   of light in the
      night sky

watching over those
   who remain

ALL HALLOW'S EVE REVERIE

This sack of a body
lies here in dawn light

Its folds, heavy,
one on the other,

Who am I underneath skin
and skeleton, the flesh
like a costume

Who will I be when
this is gone

On this day of All Hallow's Eve,
the dead, or memories of them
rise like phantasms

Intimations perhaps
of a festive future
when this familiar form
will lie empty

Today, though,
I will join the little ones,
lithe and lovely,
in ballerina dresses
and gauzy wings,

prancing and skipping,
bringing joy to every
open door

THE VILLAGE WOMAN

The village woman
who never left
looks at me with alert,
round eyes
bright in her face
of criss-crossed lines
framed by the soft
black kerchief

She pierces my gaze

I feel that I am looking
into my past,
what might have
been my fate
had my grandmother
not chosen
otherwise

Like a tiny dark mountain goat,
the woman scrambles up steep paths
that leave me breathless

She, one with the place—
I, wed to it
by memory
and history

Both of us,
part of this stone village
of our ancestors,
bound
beyond
time

CIRCLE OF BODIES

We stand
on a city sidewalk,
a circle of bodies,
arms entwined

Flesh finding flesh,
Blood finding
blood

Brother to sister
to brother
to sister

Unbroken line,
inbred with mother's
breath

For an instant,
we become again
as children
in our family garden

Cement gives way to softly
tilled earth before early
summer planting

We sink ankle deep
into grainy darkness
turned to light
by our father's hand

Like a field stretching wider
than we see, the ground
of our parents

and grandparents
draws our white feet

Sucking into the spaces
between our toes,
rooting us in mysteries

Older now,
how alike our hands,
lined, firm—the veins,
blue green rivers
of the ancestors,
gnarled connectors
watering familiar soil

THE EARTH

The surface of the earth
is thin, like skin

We seldom sense it as
so subtle, so delicate
an integument—
breathing, flowing,
flowering

Suffocating,
crusted over with
empty cans, metal,
plastic bits of litter,
it still struggles
to send forth
shoots of life

When will we learn to
tender it a gentle touch,
as if caressing a lover
who gives us food
and drink, and a
soft place to
rest

BABY BIRD

Why did this
baby bird fall out
of its nest

You'd think that
nature would
take better care
of its own,
or not . . .

A body soft, plump,
feathers still drying,
half stuck to the tiny body

Wings formed in minute
detail, the tips of feathers
protrude like tiny teeth,
according to design

Black pointed beak
efficient tool for pecking open
the semi-transparent prison
of the egg

The nest is still and silent,
now abandoned
mother bird, flown from
the disaster of her
young one's demise

I choose a spot
beneath a wild cherry,
dig a shallow grave,
nestle the limp form gently
into the soft earth

Cover it with flat stones
dry leaves, branches,
so that it blends with
all around it

My grandson, newly born,
often still curled as he was
in the womb, is now
alive and thriving

But in another country
he might have died,
transverse as he was
unable to find his
way

My daughter, too,
in another country,
could also have perished
from exhaustion, from
loss of life blood

"The way of nature"
What is the way? Why do
some live and some die,
some thrive, some fail?

A sadness fills the
stillness, a staring
into the eye of
moving clouds

I'm lost and I'm here,
suspended in the space
between birth and death,
still trying to find my way

GEMELLE

The twins are dancing,
their slender, curved bodies,
white under filmy tutus

Supple and graceful, they whirl
and reach to the strumming
beats of Italian music
on this sunny Wilbur Street
afternoon

Ava closes her eyes,
steps through space,
arms outstretched,
open to the world

Nina smiles softly,
twirls with concentration,
deep in her private world,
ending in a practiced bow

A scene of sheer magic
as they step onto
the stage of
their lives

So innocent, so pure,
they embrace the world
and are embraced
in turn

Like the crystal globe
that Nina clasps,
this moment is held
in time

Memory fixing it forever
as they two blissfully float
in the contained and golden
space of Home

gemelle—twins

ON SEEING MY MOTHER'S DRESSER AT EASTER

The mirror of the once
elegant vanity is now
mysteriously lost

Heavy dark wood furniture
with gold trim lives among
children and grandchildren

Your marriage bed, scratched
and worn by your beloved dog's
excited paws,

dwells in deep country
hundreds of miles from its
lived history

In this well of silence
you often rise
to the surface

Your gaze and smile
emanate with crystal
clarity

Where are you now?

I can summon your
memory, sense your
presence

But I can no longer
reach out
to touch you

My fingers find
only traces
on this worn wood
you left behind

TIME OF THE TURTLES

In this middle month of summer
when orange tiger lilies flower
and the flat pavement of country roads
retains heat, even at night

I often see a dark shadow in broad daylight
outlined against sun-filled asphalt
rounded form, head leading straight out
from the curved shell, pointed tail behind

Yet another tortoise striking out
from the shady edge
to cross the great black divide

Why this sudden urge to risk
what can never be
regained if lost

Each time, I wonder,
either swerving to avoid the
slow moving form or riding over it
centered between the wheels

Each time, I ruminate on
the oft too-hurried pace of life,
and its eventual demise

V: *Reflections*

HIGH DESERT

The high desert stretches flat
under the dome of sky
waiting patiently for the sun to rise
rosy in the east after the blackness
of a night unbroken by stars

I wait, wait for your presence
to fill me with golden light
wait for your warmth to flood
my blue green veins
with rivers of love

I bow under the whisper of your voice
like grasses in the dawn wind
giving myself over
to the fullness
of your generous
embrace

KEEPING COMPANY

In the middle of this dark night
I keep company with James Joyce
Saint Thomas, Proust, my father,
scribbling the lines
that Psyche proffers
only in silence,
only in solitude

When I least anticipate a visit, she comes—
a phrase, connected to a long psychic thread
pulled from the raveled skein of memory,
emerges from a forgotten abyss,
drawn by some mysterious provocation
into the semi-light
of night

I, the sleepy reluctant scribe,
hide my small electric candle under
conjugal blankets to notate, as best I can,
results of an inner reasoning, imponderable
to the day mind but beckoning through
a fog of nepenthe to be
recorded on a white page

If I do not heed the siren's call
a key phrase will be lost in the sea
of dreams and I will wake
rested but empty,
my companions, Joyce,
Saint Thomas, Proust,
my father, still sleeping
after their night labors

And so, with heavy, hooded eyes,
I scribble my small offering,
each fragile resilient strand,
part of the homespun weave
of human story

VOICE

A voice,
constrained by time,
crackles in my ear

Your cell phone,
my cell phone,
like tin cans at
the end of a
taut string

We shout to be heard,
straining to decipher
the coded message
of tender intent beneath
the multitude of syllables,
bouncing like atoms
in a universe
of space

Will we find a moment,
perhaps in shared silence,
vibrating like that
taut string,

when our words
will hum to each other,
and we will
both be satisfied
that we have heard
and been heard?

LIVING THE QUESTION

I burn the news
to give me heat

Farmers with aids
in Seixan Province,
Displaced refugees
crossing borders

Two youths face to face
Israeli and Palestinian,
pleading, one with the other,
for moderation

Kofi Annan speaks
to the import of every life

Quick flames
consume them all

Outside,
round about this simple house
ice rings each branch
fields glisten with taut
transparent skin

A small knot
in my own heart
puzzles me
with its persistence

How to create an open
space between
two people

I sit, silent,
pondering
the question

THE EVERPRESENT EYE OF GOD

Does the everpresent eye of god
look down upon these soldiers,
bare armed, carrying rifles,
marching toward their
own destruction?

And where is the
everpresent heart of god?

Does it beat more sadly
to the cries of innocents
sacrificed to greed and
blind oration?

Does the moment of death
visit god's justice
on supposed enemies,
making them equal, so that
none will ever again
kiss his wife, mother,
child?

Does the ear of god
hear the keening cries floating
through smoke sodden air?

Does the mouth of god
recite the prayer
for the dead over
the mound of
still forms under
his everpresent
eye?

A KISS ON THE LIPS

My father once
kissed me on the lips—
a shock—
each of us
recoiling at
the intimacy
of contact
then smiling together
at the "accident"

Such a surprise
in his kitchen
where he lived
with my mother
in the later years
of their long
marriage

I must have been
in my forties,
he in his late sixties,
hardly demonstrative

I can actually remember
rare contacts
of a physical nature
between us

It was a Sunday,
most likely after
one of the
longer visits,

Both of us getting older,
a growing unspoken
acknowledgement,
a growing closeness,
an appreciation

I leaned toward him
Did I raise my arms
in an embrace?
He moved toward me,
not a tall man,
but a little taller than I,
and he kissed me
on the mouth

Both of us,
moving quickly away,
laughing

Both, perhaps, delighted
at the strength
of emotion expressed,
his lips hard on mine
just for an instant

Telling me in that one
motion the depth
of his affection so rarely
even hinted at

That impression, so strong,
returns in this instant
of my own aging self

Nearly sixty-five,
I'm in my son's home,

far from the larger family,
he barely thirty nine

Have I told him often
enough how much I
love him?

Does he understand,
the shyness sometimes
between parent and
child?

Perhaps because the
bond is so deep,
so primal, it is almost
embarrassing to
acknowledge

I'm grateful, Father,
for that one unguarded
instant when you showed
me what you felt,
that instant when
we truly met

"WHERE'S ANNIE?"

The later years
she'd sit at the kitchen table
quietly, in her corner,
observing the goings on

Children grown, their children
grown, great grandchildren
parading through as if on stage
each playing a dramatic part

a book always by her side
romantic novels speaking
of betrayal and broken hearts
themes with which she
was intimately familiar

Her lifelong bluster and
opinionated views—quieted,
her eyes more clear
a smile more present

Skin tinged pink with the
finest of lines scribing her
most habitual expressions

Occasionally she would
glance up, looking for a
long concentrated moment
out the small window onto
the garden where the lily of
the valley grew in a circle

"Annie—do you see Annie?"
she'd ask, convinced that her

older sister was there, kneeling,
her diminutive barrel-shaped body
wrapped in the finely worn cotton
apron with blue printed dots

"Do you see Annie?"
in a soft affectionate voice,
the Annie she'd fought with
all her life

Gentle Annie, her nemesis,
whose nature was the complete
opposite of her own

Sweet Annie, until goaded
again and again by her younger
sister, she would finally explode,
pouring forth a volley of vile words
in a dialect only they two
deeply understood

Even grey hair did not stem
the blood lava flowing through
gnarled veins knotting them
together for over eighty years

One buried now
the other sitting in a chair
calling her name through
transparent glass

ANOINTED

He carried it throughout *l'Italia*,
the Italy he hardly knew

Pressed upon him by the village woman
who had known his grandmother

Heavy, one liter coca cola bottle filled with
dense liquid gold, now safely ensconced
in the overhead compartment of his direct
Alitalia flight back to the States

He slept dreaming of the *olivi*, ancient trees
on his plot of *terra nativa*,
the birthplace of his family
in the mountains of Irpinia

The golden liquid swelled to bursting,
as the olives had swelled beneath the
granite millstone

It dripped ever so slowly through
the tightly screwed red plastic cap,
through the folded layers
of protective wrapping, through
the crack of the locker door

Anointing his forehead with the perfume
and tears of his ancestors

Reminding him of the dreams of gold
that first brought them to *La Merica*
and the questions which had brought him
back to Italy one hundred years later

His grandfather of the stocky frame
short legs planted in the stony soil
arms made strong by fourteen daily
hours of lifting and lowering the
iron pick

Grandmother, woman of the sloping fields,
terraced in graceful arcs
by the men and women together
from rosy dawn
to blue dusk

One hundred years separated their journeys
one hundred years of three hundred and
sixty five days each

One hundred years which now
bound him intimately to them

And he understood, finally,
understood in his deepest bones,
something of the force of his
legacy, his *destino*

Rooted in the fruit of the soil
which now bathed him in its
most exquisite abundance

THE DAYS ARE LOST, COUNTING

I wake in the morning light,
assaulted too quickly by the tasks
waiting to be requited

Dawn's rosy fingers float past unnoticed,
already the day is too heavy with care

Slipping back into somnolence,
can I have another chance to waken
more fully to the day's promise,
grasping back what was so blindly lost

an openness stretching before me like fields
of snow as far as meets the gaze,
the curtain of sky still bestowing
softly falling flakes

Can this moment be the true awakening,
my breath merging with yours
as we lie silent in the soft shadows

Can I be with you as steadily
as the descending snow,
an accumulation of mornings
mounding around us

Our forms fitting the sculpture
of our lives as simply
as this

NIGHT KITTEN

The car seems to float
on the river of
dark road

Glistening lights skim
few forms as
I glide by

One lone kitten
picking her way is
the only movement
I see

Solitary, I too,
stay my course

Mind slipping
between liquid space
and memory

Holding the past
and present as close
as this wheel

Steering
towards
home

INTERLUDE

Between birth

and death

an interlude

we call

Life

WHEEL

Is it true, as
the Buddhists say,
that we're on a
wheel of life—
revolving,
evolving?

Sometimes,
as I listen
to the news
spiraling
around
the globe

I wonder if
we are
devolving?

How can we call
each other enemy
when we all love,
suffer, rejoice,
die?

Are we learning anything,
or just repeating,
repeating what
has gone
before?

The wheel turns
We turn with it

Turning
  Turning
    Turning

ACKNOWLEDGMENTS

Grateful thanks to the editors of the following publications where these poems have appeared, or are forthcoming, some in earlier versions.

Addison Independent, "Act of Faith"

Bridging the Waters I, "Night of First Snow"

Brownstone Poets, "Voice"

I-Italy, "Ballad of the Pans"

Italian Americana, "St. Mary's Church"

Shabdaguchha, "Requiem for Tsunami Dead," "Too American," "99 Cent Dreams"

I am very grateful to the Bordighera Press for making the publication of this book possible. Deep gratitude to the patient readers who revued the manuscript and to the Italian American Writers Association, Otter Creek Poets, and Stone Valley Poets for being the "testing ground" for so many of these poems, and for listening with compassionate ears. Thank you to my life partner, Woody, and to all of the members of my family, the ones who have gone before, the ones accompanying me in the present, and the newest ones—all of them my teachers; and to Kokoro Mountain Pond and my Benson studio in Vermont, as well as Angels' Landing in Provincetown, where so many of these poems were written, revised, and arranged.

ABOUT THE AUTHOR

B. AMORE is an artist, educator, and writer who has spent her life between Italy and America. She studied at Boston University, University of Rome, Accademia di Belle Arti di Carrara and is the recipient of Massachusetts Cultural grants, a Fulbright Grant, Mellon Fellowship as well as a Citation of Merit Award presented by the Vermont Arts Council. She is founder of the Carving Studio and Sculpture Center in Vermont, an international program for sculptors and co-founder of Kokoro Studio Retreat Center.

Amore taught for many years at the Boston Museum School and as an Artist Teacher and Visiting Critic with the Vermont College MFA and ADP programs. She has won numerous public art commissions in both the USA and Japan and is represented by SOHO 20 Gallery, New York and Boston Sculptors Gallery, Boston. *Life line – filo della vita*, her multimedia, six room exhibit, premiered at Ellis Island and has traveled in the US and Italy. It has been published as *An Italian American Odyssey, Life line – filo della vita: Through Ellis Island and Beyond* by Fordham Press and the Center for Migration Studies. Recent commissions include the *Centennial Collage* for Dorothea's House in Princeton, New Jersey and *Gateway, Past, Present, Future, I and II*, for Coppersmith Village, Neighborhood of Affordable Housing in East Boston. Her exhibit, *Rondini di Passaggio – Birds of Passage*, is on view at the Museo di Emigrazione in Sant'Angelo dei Lombardi, Avellino, Italy.

She has been a Featured Writer at the Italian American Writers Association, Bluestockings, Phoenix, and the Yale Club New Poetry series. Other publications include *Art by Mexican Farmworkers in Vermont, Carving Out a Dream*, and her art and poetry reviews in Sculpture magazine, Art New England, the Times Argus/Rutland Herald, and *VIA*. Her creative writing is found in *Brownstone Poets Anthology, Italian Americana, Shabdaguchha, Bridging the Waters I and II, VIA, Biancheria, Speaking Memory: Oral Culture and Italians in America, Daughters and Dads and the Path through Grief, Tales from Italian America, The Italian Americans: A History* (PBS), and *Delirious*

Naples: A Cultural History of the City of the Sun, among others. She is currently editing *Living the Dream*, a collected history of the Carving Studio and Sculpture Center, which she founded thirty-three years ago and working on a sculpture, *Arc of Healing Hands* for Tufts Medical Center, Boston, MA.

VIA Folios
A refereed book series dedicated to the culture of Italians and Italian Americans.

ALDO PALAZZESCHI. *The Manifestos of Aldo Palazzeschi*. Vol 140. Literature. $14
ROSS TALARICO. *The Reckoning*. Vol 139. Poetry. $24
MICHELLE REALE. *Season of Subtraction*. Vol 138. Poetry. $8
MARISA FRASCA. *Wild Fennel*. Vol 137. Poetry. $10
RITA ESPOSITO WATSON. *Italian Kisses*. Vol. 136. Memoir. $14
SARA FRUNER. *Bitter Bites from Sugar Hills*. Vol. 135. Poetry. $12
KATHY CURTO. *Not for Nothing*. Vol. 134. Memoir. $16
JENNIFER MARTELLI. *My Tarantella*. Vol. 133. Poetry. $10
MARIA TERRONE. *At Home in the New World*. Vol. 132. Essays. $16
GIL FAGIANI. *Missing Madonnas*. Vol. 131. Poetry. $14
LEWIS TURCO. *The Sonnetarium*. Vol. 130. Poetry. $12
JOE AMATO. *Samuel Taylor's Hollywood Adventure*. Vol. 129. Novel. $20
BEA TUSIANI. *Con Amore*. Vol. 128. Memoir. $16
MARIA GIURA. *What My Father Taught Me*. Vol. 127. Poetry. $12
STANISLAO PUGLIESE. *A Century of Sinatra*. Vol. 126. Popular Culture. $12
TONY ARDIZZONE. *The Arab's Ox*. Vol. 125. Novel. $18
PHYLLIS CAPELLO. *Packs Small Plays Big*. Vol. 124. Literature.
FRED GARDAPHÉ. *Read 'em and Reap*. Vol. 123. Criticism. $22
JOSEPH A. AMATO. *Diagnostics*. Vol 122. Literature. $12.
DENNIS BARONE. *Second Thoughts*. Vol 121. Poetry. $10
OLIVIA K. CERRONE. *The Hunger Saint*. Vol 120. Novella. $12
GARIBLADI M. LAPOLLA. *Miss Rollins in Love*. Vol 119. Novel. $24
JOSEPH TUSIANI. *A Clarion Call*. Vol 118. Poetry. $16
JOSEPH A. AMATO. *My Three Sicilies*. Vol 117. Poetry & Prose. $17
MARGHERITA COSTA. *Voice of a Virtuosa and Coutesan*. Vol 116. Poetry. $24
NICOLE SANTALUCIA. *Because I Did Not Die*. Vol 115. Poetry. $12
MARK CIABATTARI. *Preludes to History*. Vol 114. Poetry. $12
HELEN BAROLINI. *Visits*. Vol 113. Novel. $22
ERNESTO LIVORNI. *The Fathers' America*. Vol 112. Poetry. $14
MARIO B. MIGNONE. *The Story of My People*. Vol 111. Non-fiction. $17
GEORGE GUIDA. *The Sleeping Gulf*. Vol 110. Poetry. $14
JOEY NICOLETTI. *Reverse Graffiti*. Vol 109. Poetry. $14
GIOSE RIMANELLI. *Il mestiere del furbo*. Vol 108. Criticism. $20
LEWIS TURCO. *The Hero Enkidu*. Vol 107. Poetry. $14
AL TACCONELLI. *Perhaps Fly*. Vol 106. Poetry. $14
RACHEL GUIDO DEVRIES. *A Woman Unknown in Her Bones*. Vol 105. Poetry. $11

BERNARD BRUNO. *A Tear and a Tear in My Heart*. Vol 104. Non-fiction. $20
FELIX STEFANILE. *Songs of the Sparrow*. Vol 103. Poetry. $30
FRANK POLIZZI. *A New Life with Bianca*. Vol 102. Poetry. $10
GIL FAGIANI. *Stone Walls*. Vol 101. Poetry. $14
LOUISE DESALVO. *Casting Off*. Vol 100. Fiction. $22
MARY JO BONA. *I Stop Waiting for You*. Vol 99. Poetry. $12
RACHEL GUIDO DEVRIES. *Stati zitt, Josie*. Vol 98. Children's Literature. $8
GRACE CAVALIERI. *The Mandate of Heaven*. Vol 97. Poetry. $14
MARISA FRASCA. *Via incanto*. Vol 96. Poetry. $12
DOUGLAS GLADSTONE. *Carving a Niche for Himself*. Vol 95. History. $12
MARIA TERRONE. *Eye to Eye*. Vol 94. Poetry. $14
CONSTANCE SANCETTA. *Here in Cerchio*. Vol 93. Local History. $15
MARIA MAZZIOTTI GILLAN. *Ancestors' Song*. Vol 92. Poetry. $14
MICHAEL PARENTI. *Waiting for Yesterday: Pages from a Street Kid's Life*. Vol 90. Memoir. $15
ANNIE LANZILLOTTO. *Schistsong*. Vol 89. Poetry. $15
EMANUEL DI PASQUALE. *Love Lines*. Vol 88. Poetry. $10
CAROSONE & LOGIUDICE. *Our Naked Lives*. Vol 87. Essays. $15
JAMES PERICONI. *Strangers in a Strange Land: A Survey of Italian-Language American Books*.Vol 86. Book History. $24
DANIELA GIOSEFFI. *Escaping La Vita Della Cucina*. Vol 85. Essays. $22
MARIA FAMÀ. *Mystics in the Family*. Vol 84. Poetry. $10
ROSSANA DEL ZIO. *From Bread and Tomatoes to Zuppa di Pesce "Ciambotto"*.Vol. 83. $15
LORENZO DELBOCA. *Polentoni*. Vol 82. Italian Studies. $15
SAMUEL GHELLI. *A Reference Grammar*. Vol 81. Italian Language. $36
ROSS TALARICO. *Sled Run*. Vol 80. Fiction. $15
FRED MISURELLA. *Only Sons*. Vol 79. Fiction. $14
FRANK LENTRICCHIA. *The Portable Lentricchia*. Vol 78. Fiction. $16
RICHARD VETERE. *The Other Colors in a Snow Storm*. Vol 77. Poetry. $10
GARIBALDI LAPOLLA. *Fire in the Flesh*. Vol 76 Fiction & Criticism. $25
GEORGE GUIDA. *The Pope Stories*. Vol 75 Prose. $15
ROBERT VISCUSI. *Ellis Island*. Vol 74. Poetry. $28
ELENA GIANINI BELOTTI. *The Bitter Taste of Strangers Bread*. Vol 73. Fiction. $24
PINO APRILE. *Terroni*. Vol 72. Italian Studies. $20
EMANUEL DI PASQUALE. *Harvest*. Vol 71. Poetry. $10
ROBERT ZWEIG. *Return to Naples*. Vol 70. Memoir. $16
AIROS & CAPPELLI. *Guido*. Vol 69. Italian/American Studies. $12
FRED GARDAPHÉ. *Moustache Pete is Dead! Long Live Moustache Pete!*. Vol 67. Literature/Oral History. $12
PAOLO RUFFILLI. *Dark Room/Camera oscura*. Vol 66. Poetry. $11
HELEN BAROLINI. *Crossing the Alps*. Vol 65. Fiction. $14

COSMO FERRARA. *Profiles of Italian Americans*. Vol 64. Italian Americana. $16
GIL FAGIANI. *Chianti in Connecticut*. Vol 63. Poetry. $10
BASSETTI & D'ACQUINO. *Italic Lessons*. Vol 62. Italian/American Studies. $10
CAVALIERI & PASCARELLI, Eds. *The Poet's Cookbook*. Vol 61. Poetry/Recipes. $12
EMANUEL DI PASQUALE. *Siciliana*. Vol 60. Poetry. $8
NATALIA COSTA, Ed. *Bufalini*. Vol 59. Poetry. $18.
RICHARD VETERE. *Baroque*. Vol 58. Fiction. $18.
LEWIS TURCO. *La Famiglia/The Family*. Vol 57. Memoir. $15
NICK JAMES MILETI. *The Unscrupulous*. Vol 56. Humanities. $20
BASSETTI. ACCOLLA. D'AQUINO. *Italici: An Encounter with Piero Bassetti*. Vol 55. Italian Studies. $8
GIOSE RIMANELLI. *The Three-legged One*. Vol 54. Fiction. $15
CHARLES KLOPP. *Bele Antiche Stòrie*. Vol 53. Criticism. $25
JOSEPH RICAPITO. *Second Wave*. Vol 52. Poetry. $12
GARY MORMINO. *Italians in Florida*. Vol 51. History. $15
GIANFRANCO ANGELUCCI. *Federico F.* Vol 50. Fiction. $15
ANTHONY VALERIO. *The Little Sailor*. Vol 49. Memoir. $9
ROSS TALARICO. *The Reptilian Interludes*. Vol 48. Poetry. $15
RACHEL GUIDO DE VRIES. *Teeny Tiny Tino's Fishing Story*. Vol 47. Children's Literature. $6
EMANUEL DI PASQUALE. *Writing Anew*. Vol 46. Poetry. $15
MARIA FAMÀ. *Looking For Cover*. Vol 45. Poetry. $12
ANTHONY VALERIO. *Toni Cade Bambara's One Sicilian Night*. Vol 44. Poetry. $10
EMANUEL CARNEVALI. *Furnished Rooms*. Vol 43. Poetry. $14
BRENT ADKINS. et al., Ed. *Shifting Borders. Negotiating Places*. Vol 42. Conference. $18
GEORGE GUIDA. *Low Italian*. Vol 41. Poetry. $11
GARDAPHÈ, GIORDANO, TAMBURRI. *Introducing Italian Americana*. Vol 40. Italian/American Studies. $10
DANIELA GIOSEFFI. *Blood Autumn/Autunno di sangue*. Vol 39. Poetry. $15/$25
FRED MISURELLA. *Lies to Live By*. Vol 38. Stories. $15
STEVEN BELLUSCIO. *Constructing a Bibliography*. Vol 37. Italian Americana. $15
ANTHONY JULIAN TAMBURRI, Ed. *Italian Cultural Studies 2002*. Vol 36. Essays. $18
BEA TUSIANI. *con amore*. Vol 35. Memoir. $19
FLAVIA BRIZIO-SKOV, Ed. *Reconstructing Societies in the Aftermath of War*. Vol 34. History. $30
TAMBURRI. et al., Eds. *Italian Cultural Studies 2001*. Vol 33. Essays. $18
ELIZABETH G. MESSINA, Ed. *In Our Own Voices*. Vol 32. Italian/American Studies. $25
STANISLAO G. PUGLIESE. *Desperate Inscriptions*. Vol 31. History. $12

HOSTERT & TAMBURRI, Eds. *Screening Ethnicity*. Vol 30. Italian/American Culture. $25
G. PARATI & B. LAWTON, Eds. *Italian Cultural Studies*. Vol 29. Essays. $18
HELEN BAROLINI. *More Italian Hours*. Vol 28. Fiction. $16
FRANCO NASI, Ed. *Intorno alla Via Emilia*. Vol 27. Culture. $16
ARTHUR L. CLEMENTS. *The Book of Madness & Love*. Vol 26. Poetry. $10
JOHN CASEY, et al. *Imagining Humanity*. Vol 25. Interdisciplinary Studies. $18
ROBERT LIMA. *Sardinia/Sardegna*. Vol 24. Poetry. $10
DANIELA GIOSEFFI. *Going On*. Vol 23. Poetry. $10
ROSS TALARICO. *The Journey Home*. Vol 22. Poetry. $12
EMANUEL DI PASQUALE. *The Silver Lake Love Poems*. Vol 21. Poetry. $7
JOSEPH TUSIANI. *Ethnicity*. Vol 20. Poetry. $12
JENNIFER LAGIER. *Second Class Citizen*. Vol 19. Poetry. $8
FELIX STEFANILE. *The Country of Absence*. Vol 18. Poetry. $9
PHILIP CANNISTRARO. *Blackshirts*. Vol 17. History. $12
LUIGI RUSTICHELLI, Ed. *Seminario sul racconto*. Vol 16. Narrative. $10
LEWIS TURCO. *Shaking the Family Tree*. Vol 15. Memoirs. $9
LUIGI RUSTICHELLI, Ed. *Seminario sulla drammaturgia*. Vol 14. Theater/Essays. $10
FRED GARDAPHÈ. *Moustache Pete is Dead! Long Live Moustache Pete!*. Vol 13. Oral Literature. $10
JONE GAILLARD CORSI. *Il libretto d'autore. 1860 – 1930*. Vol 12. Criticism. $17
HELEN BAROLINI. *Chiaroscuro: Essays of Identity*. Vol 11. Essays. $15
PICARAZZI & FEINSTEIN, Eds. *An African Harlequin in Milan*. Vol 10. Theater/Essays. $15
JOSEPH RICAPITO. *Florentine Streets & Other Poems*. Vol 9. Poetry. $9
FRED MISURELLA. *Short Time*. Vol 8. Novella. $7
NED CONDINI. *Quartettsatz*. Vol 7. Poetry. $7
ANTHONY JULIAN TAMBURRI, Ed. *Fuori: Essays by Italian/American Lesbiansand Gays*. Vol 6. Essays. $10
ANTONIO GRAMSCI. P. Verdicchio. Trans. & Intro. *The Southern Question*. Vol 5.Social Criticism. $5
DANIELA GIOSEFFI. *Word Wounds & Water Flowers*. Vol 4. Poetry. $8
WILEY FEINSTEIN. *Humility's Deceit: Calvino Reading Ariosto Reading Calvino*. Vol 3. Criticism. $10
PAOLO A. GIORDANO, Ed. *Joseph Tusiani: Poet. Translator. Humanist*. Vol 2. Criticism. $25
ROBERT VISCUSI. *Oration Upon the Most Recent Death of Christopher Columbus*. Vol 1. Poetry.

www.ingramcontent.com/pod-product-compliance
Lightning Source LLC
Chambersburg PA
CBHW022112090426
42743CB00008B/819